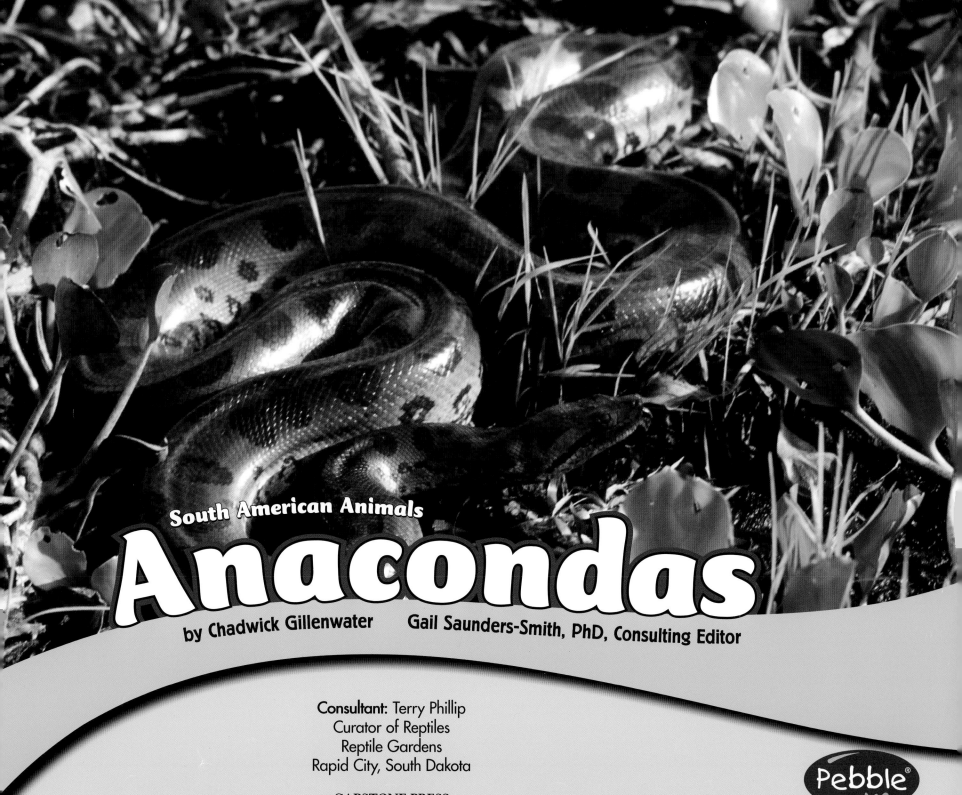

South American Animals

Anacondas

by Chadwick Gillenwater   Gail Saunders-Smith, PhD, Consulting Editor

Consultant: Terry Phillip
Curator of Reptiles
Reptile Gardens
Rapid City, South Dakota

CAPSTONE PRESS
a capstone imprint

Pebble®
Plus

Pebble Plus is published by Capstone Press,
1710 Roe Crest Drive, North Mankato, Minnesota 56003.
www.capstonepub.com

Books published by Capstone Press are manufactured with paper
containing at least 10 percent post-consumer waste.

Library of Congress Cataloging-in-Publication Data
Gillenwater, Chadwick.
  Anacondas / by Chadwick Gillenwater.
    p. cm.—(Pebble Plus. South American animals)
  Includes bibliographical references and index.
  Summary: "Simple text and photographs present anacondas, how they look, where they live, and what they do"—
Provided by publisher.
  ISBN 978-1-4296-7585-7 (library binding)
  1. Anaconda—Juvenile literature. I. Title. II. Series.
QL666.O63G55 2012
597.96'7—dc23   2011027031

Editorial Credits
Katy Kudela, editor; Lori Bye, designer; Kathy McColley, production specialist

Photo Credits
Alamy/Amazon-Images, 11; blickwinkel/Schmidbauer, cover; imagebroker, 5
newscom/ZUMA Press/Gary Braasch, 1; ZUMA Press/n27, 13
Photo Researchers, Inc/Francois Gohier, 15
Super Stock Inc./age fotostock, 17; Minden Pictures, 7, 19, 21; NHPA, 9

Note to Parents and Teachers

The South American Animals series supports national science standards related to life
science. This book describes and illustrates anacondas. The images support early readers in
understanding the text. The repetition of words and phrases helps early readers learn new
words. This book also introduces early readers to subject-specific vocabulary words, which are
defined in the Glossary section. Early readers may need assistance to read some words and to
use the Table of Contents, Glossary, Read More, Internet Sites, and Index sections of the book.

Printed in the United States of America in North Mankato, Minnesota.
102011   006405CGS12

Table of Contents

Giant Snakes

Anacondas are the largest snakes in the world. Slow on land, these snakes are fast swimmers. They speed through the Amazon River.

World Map

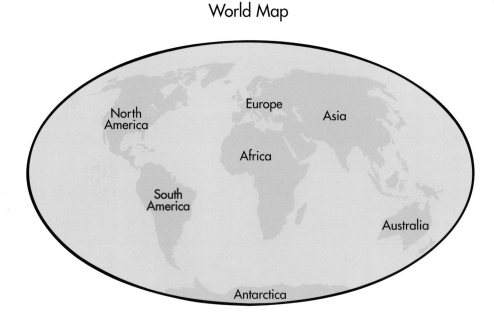

Four kinds of anacondas live in South America. These snakes spend most of their time near water. They creep through marshes looking for meals.

South America Map

 where anacondas live

Up Close!

Anacondas are heavy snakes. They weigh up to 550 pounds (250 kilograms). They stretch up to 30 feet (9 meters) long. Females are larger than males.

An anaconda's eyes and nostrils are on top of its head. The anaconda keeps its head above water and hides its body. This way prey cannot see it.

Catching Food

Anacondas catch prey by surprise. They wrap their bodies around prey and squeeze tight. They then swallow their meals whole.

Anacondas eat birds
and turtles. They catch
deer and caimans too.
One large meal can keep
an anaconda full for months.

15

Growing Up

Anacondas mate each spring. Several males will gather around a female. These males may fight one another for weeks. The female then picks a mate.

Six months later, a female gives birth to live young. The babies are born big enough to hunt. If they stay safe, anacondas live up to 40 years.

young anaconda

19

Staying Safe

Most predators stay away from grown anacondas. But ocelots and caimans hunt young snakes. To stay safe, young anacondas learn to hide in the water.

Glossary

Amazon River—the second-longest river in the world; it flows through South America

caiman—a Central and South American reptile that is related to and looks like an alligator

marsh—an area of wet, low land

mate—to join together to produce young; a mate is also the male or female partner of a pair of animals

nostril—openings in the nose used to breathe

ocelot—a wildcat of medium size with spotted fur

predator—an animal that hunts other animals for food

prey—an animal hunted by another animal for food

Read More

Burke, Johanna. *Anaconda*. Killer Snakes. New York: Gareth Stevens Pub., 2011.

De Medeiros, James. *Anacondas*. Amazing Animals. New York: Weigl Publishers, 2009.

Sexton, Colleen. *Anacondas*. Snakes Alive! Minneapolis: Bellwether Media, 2010.

Internet Sites

FactHound offers a safe, fun way to find Internet sites related to this book. All of the sites on FactHound have been researched by our staff.

Here's all you do:

Visit *www.facthound.com*

Type in this code: 9781429675857

Index

Word Count: 219
Grade: 1
Early-Intervention Level: 19